THE GIRL CODE

The Girl Code

Diane Farr

The Secret Language of Single Women

(On Dating, Sex, Shopping, and Honor Among Girlfriends)

LITTLE, BROWN AND COMPANY NEW YORK BOSTON LONDON

First Edition

Library of Congress Cataloging-in-Publication Data
Farr, Diane.
  The girl code: the secret language of single women (on dating,
sex, shopping, and honor among girlfriends) / Diane Farr;
illustrations by Diana Huff.
    p. cm.
  ISBN 0-316-26061-4
    1. Dating (Social customs) — United States.
    2. Man-woman relationships — United States.
  I. Title.

  HQ801 .F34 2001
  306.73—dc21   00-042401

10 9 8 7 6 5 4 3 2 1

PBI-IT
Printed in Italy
Designed by Leah Lococo Ltd

CONTENTS

III The Boy Code

IV The Mother Code

This Book Is Lovingly and Laughingly Dedicated to

All the Girls Who Have Helped Me Formulate

the Woman I Am Today:

Angie Gore

Lauren Bailey and Siany Davies

Lizette Diresta, Melissa Grant, and Colleen Donovan

Cooper, Anj, Laura, Trish, and Jen

Gail, Martha, and Valerie

Michelle, Becky, and Vicki

Shari, Petra, Jane, and Donna Cohen

Karen Gallagher, Rosalind, Sabrina, and Karin Graz

Nanci Ryder, Amanda Scholer, and Pam Ellis

Terri Kent and Gurmukh Kaur

Amanda Murray

Aunt Kathy, Aunt Sandy, Nena Ferriero, and Kathy Grant

Mommy and Grandma

and My Eternal Best Girlfriend:

Kristin Graziani

And the Very Special Boys Who

　　Have Reared Me to This Point,

　　for Better or Worse:

　　Michael Kernan

　　Louie Baldonieri and Barry Littman

　　Carlos, Kerry, and Omar

　　Jeff Holder, John Stevens, and Nick Kiriazis

　　Yosef Brody, Anthony Guerra, and Owen Bailey

　　David Stanley and Scott Stone

　　Michael Morrison

　　Jeradi, Bruno, Backley, Langley, Gilmore and Kelly

　　Billy, Paul Ryan, and Dad

and The Great Guy Who Told Me

　　I Should Write This Crap Down:

　　Kent Wakeford

How Do You Know a Single Girl's Home When You See One?

1. She has way too many shoes and not enough pots or pans.

2. A minimum of five products that men don't recognize are strewn around the bathroom sink.

3. There's the obligatory chair in her bedroom covered by numerous failed outfits.

4. Her fridge contains at least one alcoholic beverage, one low-calorie item, and probably not much else.

5. There are more candles than lightbulbs in every room.

6. Even if she's thirty, you can still find a packet of ramen noodles somewhere in her cabinets.

7. There is no answering machine (because she knows voice mail is more discreet).

•••

8. Somewhere there is a backpack, in case she needs to
   make use of a Eurail pass just once (or again).

9. There is a personal computer or a fax machine
   in evidence, but not a vacuum cleaner to be found.

10. There is a nightstand with a drawer, near the bed,
    to hide all sorts of things in.

(P.S. And if she's having a lucky streak, she's not there
in the morning.)

If you meet three of these requirements, don't have a wedding band, and no longer live with your parents:

then this is the book for you.

You should probably read this whole book before going
out this weekend, to remind yourself you're not alone.

Introduction

Get On

Your

Broom

and Go

．．

This handy guide and phrase book was created to unite and amuse all women by pointing out our common vocabulary — all the slang terms, euphemisms, common wisdom, and girl-speak we've picked up along the way. As such, this book is essentially an homage to friendship and should serve as a reminder that good girlfriends and laughter can get you through *anything*.

Part One of this book is a dictionary of common language that all single women share, which is born of the heartache and laughter that later we call "wisdom." It is presented here as simple terms that you and your friends might use when philosophizing about the ups and downs of the dating roller coaster that we all ride for an unspecified time. These are the homespun terms and shorthand references that you begin collecting in high school, further cultivate in college, reinvent with your first apartment roommates, and finally perfect somewhere between twenty-five and forty. Laugh with your fellow females over this vernacular we share, but don't tell the boys . . . if you give them too much information, they may use it against you later.

The Girl Code is also a long-overdue public airing of how women behave in packs — whether it be in dorm rooms or boardrooms, coffee shops or bathrooms, and a few boundaries that we need to draw between us about men.

Part Two is the implied code of behavior, ethics, and essential do's and don'ts that all you cool girls live by. As every girl knows, together we are a powerful force that abides by our own rules. If you are reading this book you've been living under these unspoken laws for at least eighteen years, but if you somehow missed out on why you keep losing girlfriends and botching up relationships, this should explain it. Welcome to the bible of being a girl's girl. These codes can and should be held against you in a court of public opinion by the sorority of sisters you hang out with.

Let's put it this way, ladies: If Lord of the Flies *was about a group of girls stranded on a desert island, Piggy would have been lynched within three days, and this book will clearly explain why.*

Most important, this book is not about how to "catch" a man. We have a deodorant made for women but we can

refuse to ever wear panty hose if we so choose. If we work hard, never marry, and renounce the right to bear children, no one will even look twice. We certainly don't need another book telling us how "tricking a man" into our lives is good for us.

This book is intended to be a sigh of relief, a reminder to all single girls that they are certainly not alone. And most of us are so by choice, whether we know it or not. This solo time in your life, dedicated just to you, should include space to make mistakes and have many more laughs with your girlfriends.

Married women will also enjoy these pages, as you recall the days before finding your soul mate, life partner, husband, or dirty old man. It's a dose of the reality of dating life and a healthy antidote to your overromanticized memories of it. You will also find that most codes of behavior between you and your girlfriends remain the same, even though your single friends tell you it's different now, just because you're off the market.

There are many definitions in this book, but let's begin with two important ones:

SINGLE: Being a single girl doesn't mean that you are loveless; it simply means that you are unmarried and that you still think of yourself first and foremost (which you have every right to do). You may be in a relationship and expect to one day marry your current date, but for the time being you don't share the same domicile or the same name with him.

GIRL: Any female who still has hopes for her future and the life force of a blooming flower is still a girl in my book (literally). As a matter of fact, my grandmother is one of the youngest girls I know.

And finally, who the hell am I? I am a single girl just like you (or the friend you will be sharing this book with) who simply took the time to write down all the best coffee-talk-philosophies I've ever heard. You know, all the war-story wisdom and homemade terms that you and all your friends, and I and all my friends, have been laughing over for years. I am also an actress you may have seen in many television shows like, *The Drew Carey Show*, *Roswell*, and *Arliss* (and hopefully by the time this is published, you'll have also seen me in a couple of good movies). Currently, I am the female star opposite Denis Leary on that "little cop show" on ABC.

But most of you will know me best from my years on that MTV show *Loveline*. Yeah, that's me, the one with the big laugh, flippy hair, and pretty strong opinions about anything I could get a word in edgewise on. After listening to 165 episodes of what's on women's minds, I know how much we really need a laugh. Playing young America's female voice on TV, giving lectures at universities across the country, and generally keeping my eyes open when I leave the house have shown me more than ever how much we also have to be thankful for.

However, what really qualifies me to write this book is the most exceptional gift I have been given: I have always been blessed with a glorious array of girlfriends. I was lucky enough to have two great brothers, but nothing in the sister department. Nothing biological, anyway . . . and I think girls who are sisterless sometimes work harder to find special women to grow up beside, all their lives. There are at least thirty-five women in my life who have saved me thousands of hours

of therapy. Actually, they are my therapy. It is they who have inspired this book and, unknowingly, coauthored it with me. We've been writing it together all my life.

And as you chuckle along with me in these pages, you will probably experience a wave of nostalgia yourself. You really should get out that address book and dial up your old friends. I believe losing girlfriends leaves a permanent scar on your soul, so I hope this inspires you to reach out and touch someone, before it's too late.

For me it's the members of "Club 66" who span from first grade to twelfth; the "B-2 warriors" in college; the "British princesses," who taught me to speak English at university; fellow "waitresses" from NYC (who are the hardest-working actresses I've ever worked with); and finally the "fab chicks" in Los Angeles that I call my closest friends, who consistently prove that real women can survive there.

1

Speaking in Code

You know those little disclaimers on the sides of cigarettes and alcohol? Well, if your next date came with a warning label, it would contain the following information down the side of his leg. This is the common language of girl-friends who've been there.

Titles

"We don't see
things as they are,
we see
them as we are."

— ANAÏS NIN

THE BOY

If you change suitors so fast that they rarely achieve name status, a man must be around for at least six weeks before you make your friends bother to learn his first name. Until such time, he should be referred to by this generic title.

For Women Who:

Need to explain to numerous people what's going
    on in their love life,

Are between the ages of sixteen and twenty-one
    or over twenty-seven,

Have overbearing mothers and aunts in their life,

Have called off more than one engagement.

As a Modifier: "It's been two months now; I think the boy has reached name status: His name is Dick, and I'm pretty sure he isn't one."

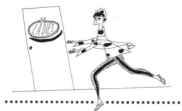

MR. RIGHT NOW

This is the guy friend of yours who doesn't have a real job,

and is always ready and available when you want

to party till dawn, and do things you wish you didn't

remember in the morning. He's not "Mr. Right,"

but he may be good enough to be "Mr. Right Now."

When to Retire Him:

Immediately after college,

When you're not so afraid of a real man,

When he asks you for cab fare home,

After a particularly lonely holiday season.

As an Excuse: "It's not that I'm afraid of a committed

relationship; at the moment all I need is to find a new

keg and to pull Mr. Right Now out from underneath

the empty one."

THE [FILL IN THE BLANK] GUY

When you've just met a man and know little to nothing about him but you need to identify him during girl talk, so you use one example of who he is, something he has, or what he does, and he becomes . . . that guy.

Best Types of References:

The kind of car he drives (*The Camaro Guy*),

His occupation (*The Personal Trainer Guy*),

Where you met him (*The Four A.M. in the Taxi Guy*),

The way in which he behaved in the morning if you've already woken up with him (*The Cuddle Guy, The Bad Breath Guy, The Up and Run Guy, etc.*).

As an Object: "He's the guy that slipped the maître d' twenty dollars for the table, spoke to the waitress like a human, and never had to use his napkin through all of dinner — you know, the Good Manners Guy."

THE TAKE-HOME PROJECT

When you feel like ignoring some larger issues in your own life, so you invest in a fixer-upper guy — who will cost you nothing but time, money, energy, and happiness. Inevitably, you learn that someone else has recouped his resale value.

Hello! You Will Never:

Fix him to your liking,

Change anything but the window dressing,

Turn him into the guy who got away,

Build the bionic man (. . . Farrah tried and she couldn't do it, even with all that hair).

As a Reminder: "Forget him, he can't even dress himself and you don't have the patience for a take-home project."

A BENEFACTOR

This is a polite title for that 35–45-year-old man who dates 19–25-year-old women. Having one always seems so original (and economical) at first, because he takes you to many more exciting places than guys your own age do and, of course, he pays for everything.
(But don't think you invented this:
In the old days they just called him a Sugar Daddy.)

Things to Look Out for:

A wife,

Some kids,

The fact that you're a grown man's Barbie doll,

That anyone who can hang out with someone who's fifteen years younger than him is a **loser**.

As a Reprimand: "No, he's not my father ... he's my benefactor; and who cares if he's bald, he pays!"

P.D.A. BOY

The guy you go out in public with and agree to hold hands with, kiss, hug, sit on the same side of the booth with, or show any other **P**ublic **D**isplay of **A**ffection, before determining boyfriend status.

Usually Causing:

Your friends to abuse you,

Your feelings for him to escalate unrealistically,

One person to suspect the other likes him or her too much too soon,

An inappropriate use of the boyfriend title or "I love you" phrase.

As an Error: "So there's me and P.D.A. boy making out in the pizza place, and in walks my boss: Kill me now."

A WELCOME MAT

This is what your friends call you when you keep
taking back the guy who only comes a-knockin'
on your door for one thing: sex, drugs, or rock 'n' roll.
(We could have just called you a doormat, but you're
always so damn friendly when he shows up.)

When Did You Decide:

To act like AstroTurf?
That he's so much better than you are?
That you didn't need therapy anymore?
That the girl who tortured you in grammar school
     was right?

As a Wake-Up Call: "Yeah, I'm sure he meant to call you,
because everyone wants to check in on a welcome mat
after they tread on it."

LUGGAGE

After you or your man has told the other to get lost
and you keep finding each other at events of mutual
interest. If you tossed him, he's the luggage, and what's
required is a game of ditch. If he tossed you, then you're
the luggage, and this is a game of looking as though
you're having a good time without him.

Necessary Requirements:

At least one ally to help you ditch or save face,

A mineral water because alcohol will kill you here,

A good seat for viewing or hiding,

A ladies' room to escape to if the game gets too intense.

As a Plea to God: "I must have 'Samsonite Customer Service'
stamped right on my forehead, because I cannot lose this
luggage for the life of me."

Types of Dates

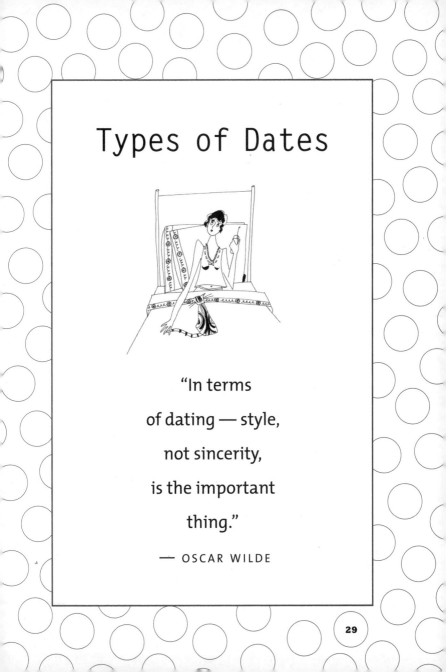

"In terms
of dating — style,
not sincerity,
is the important
thing."

— OSCAR WILDE

BOOTY CALL

This kind of rendezvous begins after one of you has already been out for the night. It starts with a post-midnight phone call that you make or receive from a place with loud music. It includes brief, often unintelligible, yet urgent conversation and ends with "See you in fifteen minutes."

Things to Keep in Mind:

The guy who's calling will never be your boyfriend,

The call itself can be seen as a symptom of alcoholism,

Don't go on this kind of date looking for a nice conversation,

This no-strings-attached encounter can nevertheless be the best reason to stay friends with ex-boyfriends.

As an Addition to Your Evening: "The phone is ringing at one A.M. . . . I'm so glad I didn't take my makeup off 'cause you just know that's a booty call."

SEMI-ANNUAL BOYFRIEND

Describes a man you see twice a year for either
Christmas and Easter, Rosh Hashanah and Passover,
Ramadan or Kwanza, or a couple of those weddings
you just can't face alone. General Rule: The less he talks,
the better it works.

Profile of This Man:

He looks good in a suit,

He understands his place,

For whatever reason, he gets your family dynamics,

He has money, or wit, or style but is missing two
     of these three.

As an Aside: "No, we're not dating, that's my semi-annual
boyfriend. Don't you remember him from the Christmas
party last year ... he owns that great tux."

SEEING-IMPAIRED DATE

Different from a blind date, this is a guy you already know, but when you met him your beer goggles were so thick that you're no longer sure what he looks like. Your fears include seeing what he looks like now, as well as seeing what you were thinking then.

Necessary Precautions May Include:

Choosing lunch instead of dinner — seeing as it's not as lengthy,

Going to a very dark bar — seeing as that's the light you probably saw him in,

Bringing the girlfriend you were with when you met him — seeing as she might recognize him,

Figuring out an escape alibi — seeing as you really have no idea what you're in for.

As Nonchalant as Possible: "Will you meet me at the restaurant at 9:30, it's a seeing-impaired date and I may need a ride to an AA meeting if my judgment was really off."

A NON-CLOSER

This is that toad you've gone out with at least three
times, and whether your intention is to suck face
or take things even further, the damn guy won't let
you close the deal. Nothing is more frustrating than
a guy that won't go there.

Possible Reasons for
His Ineptitude Include:

He's one of those misinformed boys who think nice girls
    must be virgins,

He's unable to distinguish between a lady and a nun,

He's already in love with you,

He's gay.

As a Cry of Frustration: "Where's a guy from the football
    team when you need him, I'm never going out with
    a non-closer again."

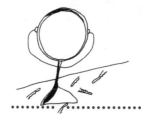

A BABY-SITTING JOB

This is a date with a man who is between three and fifteen years younger than you. Going out with him means you always plan the evenings and subsequently pay for them. (Usually you will also have to dress him, drive him, and later drop him off at his beastly apartment or parents' home.)

Why on Earth You Would Do This:

Because he's hot,

Because he's hot,

Because he's hot,

Because he's so hot, you can avoid some real big issue
    in your own life.

As a V-V-Verb: "I know you're curious about him, but please
    don't ask him to speak . . . I'm just baby-sitting him for
    a few years until he marries a supermodel."

THE PAPERWORK DATE

Not always the most romantic date, but definitely
the most modern: occurring when you and your man
have decided to have sex or to stop using condoms . . .
but you first take a little outing to the clinic together
to get your AIDS tests in unison.

Things to Keep in Mind:

Try not to have a panic attack in the waiting room
and start blurting out hundreds of names,
The pleasures that come later will greatly outweigh
this hell,
If you go together he can't chicken out, lie, and say
he did it,
Neither can you.

As an Explanation to a Married Person: "It's not weird, it's
just a paperwork date, and afterward is much better than
just going to a movie."

PLAYING HOUSE

When it's too early in the dating process to do those
things you miss most when you're single: staying home,
cuddling up, and watching a movie on the couch . . .
but the weather is so damn perfect for it that you just
do it anyway.

Best Kinds of Weather for It:

The first snowfall in the Midwest,

Early November on the East Coast,

A midsummer thunderstorm in the South,

Any third date you manage to get in the Los Angeles area,
 no matter what the weather is doing.

As a Sentence to Later Regret: "I'd actually prefer just
playing house tonight; we'll always have time for dancing
later on."

AN INDEPENDENT ACTIVITIES EVENING

When you've been dating for a long while and he wants to see you but you need to get some stuff done. Rather than reject him, you just invite him to bring his own stuff over, and both of you do your own "stuff," but in the same room. (P.S. After marriage this is called quality time.)

Perfect for:

A guy who always wants to be around,

Nights when you can't be bothered to put on makeup,

Ensuring a sleepover at your house,

Anal-retentive organization freaks who need a lot
of time at home.

As a Bargaining Chip: "C'mon honey, I'll go to your firm dinner party tomorrow if we can have an independent activities evening tonight."

Stages

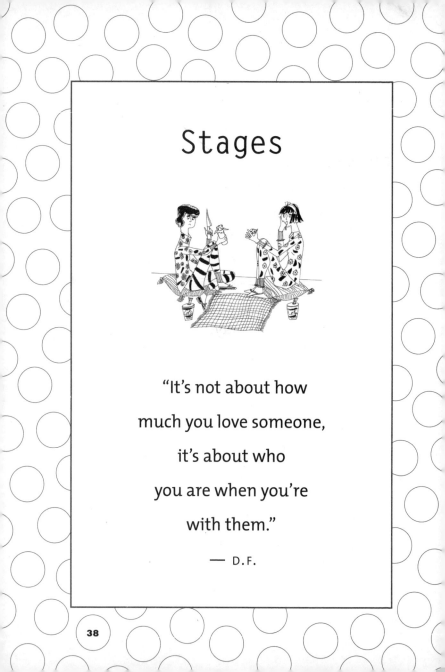

"It's not about how
much you love someone,
it's about who
you are when you're
with them."

— D.F.

DUNGEON LOVE

When your first encounter with a new lover unexpectedly lasts three days straight, causing the most intense, passionate, overwhelming, fairy-tale feelings of love ...
until you leave the house and the reality sets in that you don't know diddly squat about him in the real world.

Reasons to Do It Anyway:

Real-life love is much dimmer than dungeon love,
It's usually the most amazing sex of your life,
It's a twice-in-a-lifetime opportunity at the most,
No man will ever be perfect in the real world, so live
the fantasy while you can.

As a Confession: "On a blind date Friday night I cooked dinner for this guy from the Swedish Olympic team, and when we finally got dressed on Monday morning, I knew it was dungeon love."

IN THE ROTATION

The appropriate description of the man you see:

(1) between one and three times a month,

(2) for scheduled events rather than just hanging out,

(3) who has yet to see anything but your best behavior,

(4) who firmly believes you have no intention of
advancing your relationship beyond this status,
regardless of whether or not this is true.

Best Utilized:

When you refuse to bring up the boyfriend title until he does,

When dates are scarce and you're feeling lazy or horny,

When you can't choose between him and another
imperfect suitor,

When you don't really like him but your mother does.

As a Preposition: "We did some kissing after the movie last
week and next Friday he invited me square dancing . . .
so he's in the rotation; now we'll see how it goes."

SIAMESE

When you've been seeing a man for more than a week, but less than two months, and are so attached at the hip that you spend at least five nights a week with him. (A good indication that you've entered the Siamese stage: your girlfriends stop calling.)

Women Who Need to Monitor This Behavior:

Girls who dropped all their friends in high school every time they had a boyfriend,

Women who believe they are at least fifteen pounds overweight,

Women who haven't had a relationship in eight months,

Anyone over twenty-seven years old.

As a Dagger: "Don't even bother inviting her, she has a two-week boyfriend and is so Siamese that she checks in with him to urinate."

THE BAD HYGIENE STAGE

When you wake up with a guy on Sunday morning and neither of you bothers to shower or shave. This is a sign of a long-term thing. But remember, let this stage get out of hand and you risk killing all romance.

Do Not Attempt:

Not brushing your teeth,

Picking your nose,

Running out of toilet paper,

Farting and not even bothering to apologize.

(These things can only be accomplished by married people.)

As a Justification: "We're at the bad hygiene stage; I probably won't do a bikini wax all winter."

THE PRIDE PERIOD

The point in a relationship when you come to realize
that it is unsalvageable. Ladies, if you can't save your
relationship save your pride — it may be the only thing
you have left when it's over.

Reasons to Find the Strength:

It may take six months to get over him but it can take
years to recoup your pride,

Therapy is expensive,

Crap never gets easier to swallow,

You lived for years before him, and pride will get you
through the coming years without him.

As a Place: " I cried all night long while I packed my things;
I am finally entering the pride period."

RAW COOKIE DOUGH TIME

When you've been dumped by your man and need to lie in bed and cry for a day or two. The best thing to have on hand is one girlfriend, two spoons, and raw cookie dough ready to be eaten right out of the package.

Try This Only at Home Because:

You should never let 'em see you sweat,

Eating raw cookie dough in public grosses people out,

It's always better to hash it out before you get on with it,

If you eat the whole package, your stomach will hurt

too much to think about him.

As a Plea: "He just called me and told me we're through; please come over, it's raw cookie dough time."

BOYFRIEND HEAVEN

At the final stage of any relationship, this is the special place where the non-keepers go. Men don't break up with you, they just go to boyfriend heaven.

Helps You to:

Save face,

Imply that he's either a treasured memory or fresh roadkill,

Deflect concern, scrutiny, or pity from the peanut gallery,

Say nothing if you can't say something nice about someone.

As a Place: "I'm sure he's well, but I really wouldn't know — he's in boyfriend heaven now."

THE RECYCLING BIN

Women in the extreme stages of single life start looking for men here: the section of your address book where you keep old boyfriends' phone numbers — and occasionally rationalize that it's okay to date them again.

Occurring When Your Ex-Boyfriend Is:

Extremely handsome,

Exceptionally well endowed,

Rich as hell, or

When you need a date and are worried about adding another number to the reject list.

As an Excuse: "Don't get too attached to my date; he's from the recycling bin and won't be around for long."

Long-Distance Operators

"Sometimes I wonder if men
and women really suit each other.
Perhaps they should live next door
and just visit now and then."

— KATHARINE HEPBURN

CITY OR STATE TITLES

When the guy you are considering/smooching/ doing lives farther than one hour away, it is unlikely that your friends will ever see him, so don't expect them to remember his name. Instead, decide early on if the city or state he lives in is more impressive, and go with that one.

Upgrades in Pretension Are:

A "Seattle boy" is much more exciting than a
"Washington State guy,"
"New York man" cleverly hides the fact that he's actually
from upper Westchester County,
No one gushes for the farm guy in the next county,
but "Rolling Hills retreat boy" is fun,
And best of all: "spicy Italian man" could live in a shack
in Europe, but hey, it's still in Europe.

As an Admission: "He may be an unemployed surfer from Orange County, but my 'California dream boy' has the best state title this side of the Mississippi River."

A LOVE FEST

This is the single best reason to date an out-of-town man: the weekends away in strange and romantic places where neither of you lives. Pack lots of pretty things and prepare to show them all off.

Things to Consider in Advance:

Frequent flyer miles were actually invented for this,

Pack an excessive amount of undergarments as well as

Every shoe you own so you're prepared for anything,

Anything you do outside of your own state does not

count morally.

To Instill Jealousy in Friends: "Island boy sent me first-class tickets, so I'll be having a love fest in the Keys this weekend — I think that calls for the bikini."

DRIVE-BY DIALING

Remember the old days of calling your faraway guy late at night and hanging up when he answers ... just to make sure he is there? Well, welcome to the world of Caller ID and *69. There is no longer anything anonymous about this.

If You Really Need to Call Anyway:

Be prepared to talk, or to leave a message that you've just dreamt that he died, and he needs to call you back tonight no matter what time he gets in.

If He's on to You Doing This and You Really Can't Get Caught Again:

Just do it from a pay phone.

From a Reformed Check-In Junkie: "I tried a drive-by dialing last night, and let me tell you how badly I got busted trying to pull away."

D.W.I.

Different from a booty call, **D**ialing **W**hile **I**ntoxicated to far-away attractions leads to nothing but bad conversation, often a crying jag, and always a hefty phone bill fine at the end of the month. **Note to Self:** Just go to bed.

Keep in Mind:

Long-distance relationships and alcohol don't mix well,
You're never as attractive as you think you are when
    you're drunk,
You will probably misremember the entire conversation
    come morning,
Making sure your brain is engaged before calling a lover
    anywhere is always a good idea.

As a Concern: "After the party I went home and did a D.W.I. to Texas, and I sure hope that was a heifer I heard laughing in the background."

PHONIN' O'S

When you can't take your out-of-town lover to bed with you, you can always take him to bed via phone. If talking dirty works for you but you haven't done this before, your phone conversations are about to get a lot more interesting.

Notes to Self:

He will never see how red your face is when you first try this,

Shut off the lights if you embarrass easily,

Remember that practice makes perfect,

This is not the time to worry about the size of your phone bill.

As a Compliment: "Chicago man keeps me happy with phonin' O's, and I don't even have to put up with the terrible weather there."

A WEB MAN

One of the worst Y2K glitches reported are these new
boyfriends that people make over the Internet.
Warning: This is not an ideal place to look for romance
no matter what the commercials tell you.

Let's Be Real:

People that look like models don't go lookin' for love
at a computer terminal,
That cool guy you just met is probably four thirteen-
year-old girls laughing their asses off,
Colleges that advertise on TV are worthless; this guy
with a Web site is one step below that,
The only thing you really know about him is that
he can type.

As a Defeat: "Web man's not working out so well, his e-mail
address connected directly to the FBI today."

MANDATORY VACATIONS

When you no longer leave town whenever you want
and no longer go wherever you want because wherever
the hell that boy lives and whenever the hell he sends
a ticket is exactly where and when you'll be going.

Yes, There Are Bad Points, but Let's Look at the Good Ones:

Airline tickets are the world's greatest presents,

You're still getting out of town,

You only have to shave as often as you fly,

Lots of women go on vacation looking for a guy,

and you always find yours as soon as you land.

As a Point of Perspective: "I'm not flying anywhere else this
month; my mandatory vacations have already filled up my
out-of-town quota."

HOME TEAM SCRIMMAGE

When you start to believe that your weekend play-dates could become a real relationship and one of you invites the other to visit his or her home for an extended period so you can play house for a while. This is a warm-up game before the official season begins.

Things to Expect:

If you make a ton of plans, expect to cancel half of them,
When you need half an hour alone, ask for it politely,
    or expect to be left alone permanently,
If you don't introduce him to the people you always talk
    about, expect him to take a walk,
If he doesn't introduce you in return, expect to find
    a local girlfriend somewhere.

As a Cautionary Tale: "I had a home team scrimmage last week at his house and got a reality check: I learned he still lives with his parents."

Seasonal Lovers

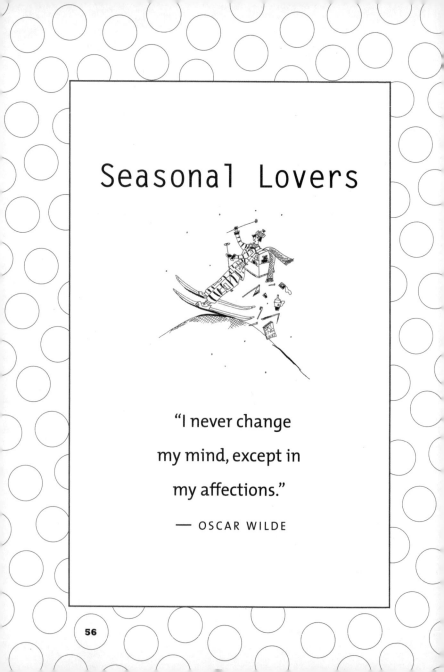

"I never change

my mind, except in

my affections."

— OSCAR WILDE

··

SUMMER LOVE

The kind of guy you really want to date when the
weather is warm, but who loses his appeal when his tan
fades. He doesn't have to be a brain surgeon, but he certainly needs to be hot.

His Usual Attributes Include:

A convertible,

A lifeguarding job,

A great upper body,

An undergraduate degree (in about two years when
he finishes school).

As Words to Make Your Mouth Water: "So I laid out my towel
right next to my summer love, and he began rubbing in
my sunscreen without saying a word."

A FALL NESTER

The kind of man you can see yourself settling down with for a few months of winter hibernation. Everyone wants someone to cuddle up with on those coming cool nights, so we go into search mode about Labor Day.

Idyllic Dates in This Season Include:

Kicking fallen leaves in the park,

A game of touch football in a turtleneck sweater,

Hot chocolate or cider after a romantic movie,

A long Thanksgiving weekend (if you make it that far).

As a Whisper: "I don't know if we'll make it to Christmas, but I saw that beard when I registered for fall classes and knew he was a fall nester."

CLUB MED MORALS

When you take a vacation in a place that creates a little fantasy world for you, and your inhibitions never make it past the baggage claim. They really should advertise these highlights in the brochure.

How Is It That:

This never-never land has so many hot guys?

These little beads manage to get you so drunk?

You never want to do any of these things when you have a boyfriend?

Guilt doesn't exist on these islands?

As a Pact with a Vacation Roommate: "I swear I'm not like this at home; they must put something in the food that gives you Club Med morals."

INSTRUCTOR BOY

The kind of romance you have while learning some
sport, during some lost weekend, that completely typifies
whatever season it's in with a guy you would otherwise
never date.

Everyone Should Have at Least One:

Ski instructor guy one winter,

Surfer/jet skier/yacht racing dude one summer,

Fly fisherman or mountain-climberman one fall,

Baseball or basketball player one spring.

P.S. You get extra points if he is a professional at
his sport or taking a year off from school
to do it full-time.

As One to Remember: "I had this instructor boy one winter
who taught me hunting up north . . . we saw all kinds
of animals and never left the cabin."

WINTER WONDER BOY

When it's so cold out that you don't want to leave

the house, and he just makes that so damn easy.

Keep the heat high, the big meals coming, and

the body heat between you.

Things to Beware of:

Gaining twenty pounds lounging around with

your teddy bear,

Worrying about where this is going when the snow melts,

Considering getting out of this before the holidays,

Neither of you shaving for two to three months.

As a Source of Warmth: "I haven't been out partying in

months, it's too cold out there and I've already got winter

wonder boy in here."

SPRING CHICKEN

This is not a type of guy, but a kind of attitude. It's the spring in your step when spring is in the air and the panic in your mind of being tied down for the summer. So, as not to get involved, you look for the friskiest guy around and start planning your spring break.

Don't Sweat the Fact That:

He'll probably never see Memorial Day,

Your parents would hate him,

He suggested Fort Lauderdale as a romantic getaway,

That your best conversations are usually over beer.

As a Personal Mantra: "So what if I'm a spring chicken and too afraid to let him in, if it's meant to be, I'll catch up with him next September."

A MIDNIGHT SNACK

This is the guy you grab on New Year's Eve for the
twelve o' clock drop. Sometimes he's grabbed just days
before, and sometimes he's grabbed right on the spot,
because let's face it, anyone will do after all that cheap
champagne.

Just Don't Stoop so Low as to Grab:

Some young'un so young he still believes in Santa,

Someone else's full-time snack,

The guy who just threw up,

Your girlfriend unless you mean it.

As Something You Will Later Admit: "He was just
a midnight snack; I really shouldn't have kept him
around till breakfast."

BIRTHDAY ICING

This guy is similar to a midnight snack but appears

only on your birthday. The same rules apply.

(Ah, what the hell, you'll have a real date next year.)

At Least Follow These Guidelines:

Don't accept expensive gifts from him,

Don't ditch him in the corner if you're throwing a party,

Don't lead him to believe this expression of loneliness

is actually deep affection,

Don't return his call next year if you're still this pitiful.

As a Wish When You Blow Out the Candles: "Please don't

let the birthday icing find out that he's only a party decora-

tion."

Before, During, and After

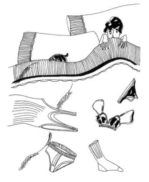

"I used

to be Snow White,

but I drifted."

— MAE WEST

THE EDDIE MONEY EXPERIENCE

When a person you are interested in merely looks at you for an extra-long moment, or perhaps holds your hand, or makes any other minor gesture in your direction, and your entire body shakes.

Necessary Reference:

Go back to your early-eighties collection of music and find "Shakin'" by Eddie Money.

As an Adjective: "The opening credits of the movie hadn't even finished when he took my hand and I had the Eddie Money experience."

REMNANTS

Those love tokens a man leaves on your body usually around your neck or shoulders that we called "hickeys" in junior high school. For the record: After eleventh grade, these are no longer cool.

Seriously, Girls:

Don't let anyone mark you as his territory,

You're allowed to make out now, so there's nothing
to prove,

Evidence of any kind can only hurt you,

The neck is the wrong area of the body for him
to be spending that much time on.

As a Woman Who's Been Had: "He can't make it up here for graduation weekend, so he left these damn remnants all over me to make sure everyone knows I'm off-limits."

ROLLING O'S

The wonderful (and, for most of us, unlikely) experience
of multiple orgasms in one lovemaking session.

Usually Only Attained:

When you've had between one and three glasses of wine,

When it's between one and three A.M. or P.M.,

When you're with a partner that you just met, or

Someone you've really done your homework with.

As a Noun, Noun, Noun: "Oh, I will never leave him — we're
talkin' rolling o's!"

WAR WOUNDS

These are the slight aches, pains, and little bruises that come from an exuberant encounter with the opposite sex. Injuries should not be permanent or require hospitalization but should bring a sideways smile to your face every time one of them acts up.

Hard-Core War Wounds May Include:

Scratches down the back,

Bruising and pinch marks down the arms and legs,

Bite marks and soreness around the chest and neck,

Rope burns, anywhere.

In the Shower to Yourself: "What the hell? ... Oh ... [Laugh] ... Ah, war wounds ... [Laugh again]"

A FIRE-DRILL F**K

The insulting attempt of a man to leave his pants around one or both ankles while making love to you, for no apparent reason other than fear of a fire drill.

Best Course of Action to Take:

Feign headache,

Show dramatic signs of fatigue,

Explain that you are experiencing a "female problem"
    and can't participate,

Immediately tell the story of the best lover you ever had.

As a Verb: "As soon as you started preparing for a fire-drill f**k, my head just started to pound — all I can hear are my mother's words about waiting."

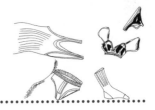

. . . .

CEILING FRIGHT

When you wake up in the morning, open your eyes wide, and think, "OH MY GOD, this is not my ceiling!" (Usually followed by a look to the left . . . you find nothing familiar . . . a look to the right . . . you find him, vaguely familiar.)

Occurring Mostly:

At state colleges,

At private colleges,

All universities,

Right before the period of self-loathing.

As a Request: "Can you please come pick me up? I've just had the worst case of ceiling fright and I don't think I can drive."

Hairy Situations

"Do you love
me because I'm beautiful
or am I beautiful
because you love me?"

— CINDERELLA

CIRCLE K

That special circle at the crown of the male's head where
he begins losing his hair. Touch it with just one finger,
and you will kill his self-esteem.

Best to Use if:

He orgasms and you don't,

He forgets something that's important to you,

He checks out every woman who passes by,

He worries about your mother being overweight.

As an Equalizer: "So 'Barbie' walks by us and he thinks he's
cool because she winked at him — I told him how cute
that was while lightly petting the circle k — that brought
him right back to reality."

RUG BURN

(Not what you're thinking.) When you've been making out with a man who didn't bother to shave, and you've kissed him for so long that the hair growth on his face has taken most of the skin off of yours.

This Is Particularly Hazardous:

If you have particularly delicate skin,

If you like southern European or Middle Eastern men,

If you have a job interview the next day,

If you are cheating on someone.

As a Lasting Memory: "No, it's not a bad facial, it's just a little rug burn — and when you see the Greek god who gave it to me, you'll know why it was worth it."

AFTERGLOW

(No, not what you're thinking either.) This occurs after
a woman gets waxing or electrolysis to remove hair from
parts of her body where polite society presumes she never
had it. It looks particularly special above one's mouth.

Ranging from:

A slight pink hue around your brows or lip,

Chicken pox down your lower legs,

Temporary third-degree burn scars around your chin,

    breasts, or stomach . . .

All, depending on how genetically cursed you are.

As an Adjective: "No, he doesn't beat me, I just have a little
afterglow going today."

SPROUTS

Those little gray hairs that you start finding that not only differ in color but in direction, too. They seem to sprout straight up from the top of your head, then curl out in every direction.

It Has Been Said:

It's better to cut them than to pull them,

It's better to color them with hair dye than to color them in with marker,

It's better to deal with them than to ignore them,

It's better to get over them now, 'cause this is just the beginning.

As an Exasperation: "As if I didn't have enough to be angry at my mother for, I'm only twenty-two and already I have sprouts!"

MIND THE GAP

Not only the distance between the train and the platform, this is also the distance between your head and the colored part of your hair. The gap between, which is your actual hair color, is not supposed to show. Go dye one section or the other.

Go Mind to It Before It's Too Obvious:

There's no point in changing to a new you if everyone
   can still see the old you,
Blondes (not used-to-be blondes) have more fun,
Highlights are supposed to start high,
Roots are supposed to stay below ground.

As an Appointment to Keep: "I really have to mind the gap this weekend before the colors on my head look like an African flag."

Fighting

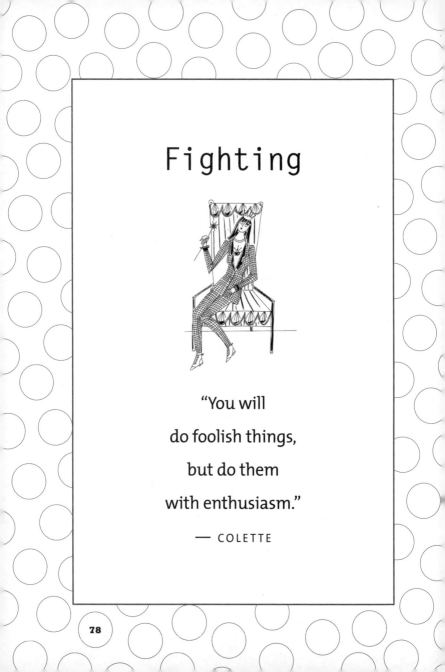

"You will

do foolish things,

but do them

with enthusiasm."

— COLETTE

THE JUDAS KISS

When your lover is guilty of something and plants a kiss on your cheek, just as Judas did when he turned on his Almighty One. Watch him, woman, he's up to something. (If flowers or other unprompted gifts accompany this kiss, you are in serious trouble.)

Things to Assess:

Your phone bill and credit card statement for any
   unauthorized purchases,
Whether there are engagements coming up that
   he doesn't want to attend,
Where he was all day,
Most important, where he was last night.

As an Omen: "He walked into the dinner party late, made big apologies to everyone, and planted a Judas kiss right on my forehead. Something's up."

TIARA TIME

The point at which your lover makes you mad enough
that you reach into an imaginary jewelry box, put on the
tiara you deserve — and let him know what a princess you
really are. Wear it well, honey, and let him have it.

When to Put It on:

If he's unsure whether you should attend a business
dinner as his date,

If he believes it's fine to go out with his ex on a
Saturday night,

When you've witnessed excessive flirting with another
woman,

If he watches three sporting events in one day.

As a Warning: "He told me I should put on more makeup
to go out to dinner with his friends — well, that just set
off tiara time."

CHEERLEADING

When your date is driving like Speed Racer and you're
so panicked that your life might end that your limbs are
flailing around madly. To onlookers it must seem that your
favorite team is playing, because you're bouncing around
like on hell of a cheerleader.

You Should Probably:

Tell him to slow down before you cramp up,

Explain that whatever he is racing to isn't worth it,

Advise him your sex drive will be functioning in direct
correlation to the brake,

Get the hell out of the car and walk if none of this works.

As a Last Confession: "I didn't try out for cheerleading
in high school for a reason, so unless you want an imaginary pom-pom to knock you out, you better slow down."

A TOURETTE'S MOMENT

The point in an argument when you are so angry and
frustrated that you blurt out information you really
never meant to share. No matter how hard you backpedal,
those words are never coming back.

Particularly Damaging Information Is:

That your ex was bigger/stronger/better,

That you never really liked his mother anyway,

That you have made out with his best friend,

That you know he's wearing a hairpiece.

As an Explanation of Why You Broke Up: "During a fight this
morning I had a Tourette's moment and told him that I've
been faking all my orgasms. I'm in big trouble."

APHRODISIACS

When you are at fault in the argument and can't bring
yourself to apologize, you can always employ an aphro-
disiac like alcohol to help divert his attention from anger
to sex. This is most effectively used after the argument
is over but while you are still in trouble.

Reasons to Reach for the Aphrodisiacs:

Sorry seems to be the hardest word,

Men believe good sex is better than an apology,

A decent bottle of wine costs eight dollars and an apology
    may cost millions,

It's hard to keep raw oysters fresh in case of an argument.

As a Noun: "So I spent the rent on a new dress, what's
the big deal? I'll slip him a couple of aphrodisiacs and
all will be forgotten."

AN EMERGENCY "I LOVE YOU"

Warning: To be used only in dire circumstances. If you really have pushed him too far and have not yet professed your love, saying "The Phrase" for the first time will immediately put him in a state of temporary insanity, leaving you forgiven of all wrongdoing.

Be Careful of:

Employing this too early and leading him to believe
that you are not only wrong but crazy, too,
Making him think you are pregnant,
Allowing him to believe you're his love slave,
Using this in a relationship that is too fleeting
for such extreme action.

As an Out: "I was really busted big-time, but I employed an emergency 'I love you' and all was forgiven. That was close!"

THREE THINGS

If you've just exchanged some verbal blows but you don't want the battle to escalate into full-blown war, you can make a peace offering of sharing three things that you really like about him and then asking him to do the same.

The Rules Are as Follows:

Emphasize one of his traits that is sweet and kind,
Compliment him on something that has nothing
to do with the argument,
Reveal something you truly admire about him that
you've never mentioned,
Listen very carefully to the three he tells you, as they
are the key to making everything all better.

As a Cry for Help: "I understand you didn't mean to insult me, but you did, and now we need to do three things before I insult you back."

Gifts

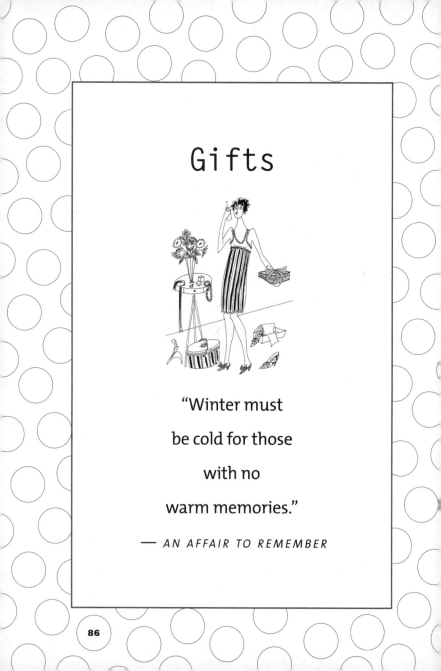

"Winter must

be cold for those

with no

warm memories."

— *AN AFFAIR TO REMEMBER*

BIG-TICKET ITEM

That very special gift that costs him enough money
or pain to immediately spring him from the doghouse.
Size of gift varies according to geographic location.

Here's a Rough Estimate:

In the Midwest:	priced usually between $100 and $250,
On either coast:	priced usually between $300 and $800,
In LA or NYC proper:	priced usually between $1,000 and $3,000,
On Long Island:	$5,000 minimum, or something the neighbors will see in the driveway.

As an Object of His Affection: "Everything's fine now. He
knows he's wrong, I got a big-ticket item this morning."

AN AMNESIA STONE

Given when you've reached that point in your relationship when you're expecting an engagement ring. You open up an expensive-looking box to find any piece of jewelry — other than a diamond — that is so big you're supposed to forget about expecting a proposal.

It Better Be:

Absolutely huge,

As expensive as the engagement ring would have been,

Worth giving him six more months to bite the bullet,

Flattering enough to call off your mother.

As a Modifier: "No, I didn't get a ring, but this tennis bracelet is working wonders as an amnesia stone."

CODEPENDENT PRESENT

When your lover is an avid sports fan and buys you lessons or equipment so you can spend your weekends doing what he likes. Keep in mind: Even if you don't share his enthusiasm for this hobby, playing with your man will prevent him from playing with other chicks when you're not there.

Typical Types:

Scuba lessons from your guy at the beach,

Tennis instruction from your blue blood in the Northeast,

Hiking boots from your Midwestern man,

Whips, chains, or handcuffs from that weirdo
in the West Village.

As an Answer to Why: "It's actually just a codependent present for him, not me — but what the hell, every girl should know how to ride a dirt bike."

P.M. PRESENTS

These are the sexy underwear ensembles that a man gives to you in the hopes of seeing you in them later. They represent the ultimate in pleasure for the gift giver and the ultimate pain in the ass for you.

Usually Something Like:

Dental floss underwear for your birthday,

The one-piece lacy freezing satin thing for the
Christmas season,

A black panty set that looks lumpy underneath
your New Year's dress,

Valentine's Day stockings with garters that fall down
as soon as you're in public.

As an Eye-Opener: "Last night we tried out his P.M. present, and now I know why those catalog models are always pouting."

OFF THE SHOPPING LIST

Those practical gifts that are completely unromantic
but totally needed in your house or apartment. You know,
those things you've been meaning to spend your own time
and money on, but having him spend his works
for both of you.

Notable Shopping List Items Include:

Lighting fixtures that you can't put up by yourself,
Pieces of furniture from stores that won't deliver,
Drills, hammers, screw guns, and other manly items
    he wants to buy anyway,
Expensive kitchen appliances that you keep borrowing
    from married friends.

In His Defense: "It's not that he didn't do any planning; I've
    needed to spackle the bathroom forever, so I asked for an
    off-the-shopping-list love token."

PHONED IT IN

When your lover didn't put any thought or care into your gift, and at the last second sent over a cheesy flower arrangement or any other one-size-fits-all-women gift, hoping you wouldn't notice.

Particularly Insulting Twists Include:

Receiving the same mail-order scarf/teddy bear/whatever that he gave his mom last year,

Carnations of any kind, or any color, even if real flowers surround them,

Those flower arrangements that go for a reduced rate because they're going to die in two hours,

Recognizing his assistant's handwriting on the card.

As a Retaliation: "He can kiss my ass for his birthday, 'cause he totally phoned it in on mine."

TRAINING WHEELS

What look like 1- to 2-karat diamond studs that are given
to you by a family member with poor taste or bought,
in desperation, for yourself. In reality, they are the sadness
stone: cubic zirconium.

Reasons to Have Them:

It's important to practice with training wheels
        to get better at the real thing,
It worked when you were five and really wanted
        a ten-speed,
It keeps a birthday gift suggestion directly in his line
        of sight,
Flaunt 'em if you got 'em and fake it if you don't, sister.

As an Object of Desire: "No, they're actually just training
wheels, but feel free to upgrade me at any time."

LATE FEES

The penalty automatically applied when your significant
other makes you feel insignificant by forgetting your
birthday or anniversary. Gifts received post–event day
must automatically double in value.

Enforcement Tactics Include:

Simply asking for the credit card,

Heading immediately to the most overpriced
store in town,

Showing up at his office with several fabulous items
and asking which one he wants to buy for you,

Giving him the number where you can be reached
on the island you'll be visiting next weekend.

As an Object of Need: "It's okay, honey, I know you love me,
and the jeweler we're meeting tomorrow knows the late
fees will apply."

When the Fat Lady Sings

"When one

door of happiness

closes,

another opens."

— HELEN KELLER

OUT OF THE CAR

When it's almost done, but not done yet, and you start warming yourself up to the idea of your life without him ... he's out of the car. Girl, it will be okay, just shut the door behind him.

Things to Remember:

All the stuff you haven't had time to do lately,

The things you never really liked about him,

That other guy you liked and tried to ignore,

Everything happens for a reason.

As a Resolution: "Forget about it; I'm not putting up with this crap anymore — he's out of the car!"

ON THE CURB

When it's really done and he's so far out of the car, that he's out the door and on the street. You, my friend, are driving away and waving to his ass sittin' on the curb. This is the time to roll up the windows, turn on the radio, and step on the gas.

Just Keep Telling Yourself:

You never have to make this mistake again,
Every wrong guy gets you one step closer to the right one,
The biggest sin in life is choosing unhappiness,
One day he'll be a funny anecdote to laugh about with
    your girlfriends.

As a Daily Mantra: "He's on the curb, and I have a green light to proceed full speed ahead."

SELF-SABOTAGE

A self-destruct mechanism usually tripped when your guy is okay but your self-esteem is not. A woman will kill a relationship just to prove she is unworthy of it. It's time to stop setting up those "imaginary windows" that are too small for him to crawl through just so you can slam them shut on yourself.

Symptoms to Look Out for:

Never being satisfied,

Relying on him to supply your happiness,

Feelings of overwhelming jealousy, fear, and anger,

Never finding the time to deal with all that "baggage"
you keep carting around.

As an Opening Line When Meeting Your Therapist:

"It's really not his fault, we just had our three-month anniversary, and my self-sabotage alarm went off to destroy the whole deal."

A DISPLACEMENT ROMANCE

When your affections for one man are displaced right
into the hands of another. This is when one relationship
breeds the next. This is not an ideal place to start a new
relationship, but an easy way to get out of your last.

What You Should Beware of:

Not facing the fact you screwed up the last one,

Simply making this relationship an extension of the other,

Giving yourself too much crap about being involved

    again so soon,

Thinking you have a realistic chance here.

As a Concession: "Yes, honey, it was a displacement romance,
but this is when I was most ready for you."

WOMB MODE

Occurs immediately after a breakup. Characterized
by a compulsion to lay on your couch in a fetal position
and the illogical desire to crawl back where you came
from and make all this go away. But if Momma can get
through labor, you can get through this. (Refer to Raw
Cookie Dough Time for additional help.)

Things to Stay Away from:

Listening to the radio — those love songs are not about you,

Visiting your old hangouts — they will only dramatize
the pain,

Watching too much TV — this can cause emotional
cancer,

The ex himself (self-explanatory).

As a Cry of Self-Pity: "No, I'm just going to stay home;
I'm in womb mode. Call me in a week."

GIRL PATROL

When your girlfriend is in the dumps because her man left her there, and you step up to the plate to take her out on the town where she belongs. Remember the importance of karma: You may need someone to do this for you one day.

What to Do with Your Friend:

Take her to lunch with that otherwise unacceptable
   guy who has a crush on her,

Vehemently diss her ex (if you're absolutely sure
   he's not coming back),

Go out dancing at a nightclub and make sure she
   only drinks water,

Put her in that wet T-shirt contest she secretly dreams
   of and boo the other contestants mercilessly.

As an Explanation: "No, John, I'm not cheating on you, my roommate's been dumped and I'm on girl patrol tonight."

CRYING WOLF

When you've broken up and gotten back together with him so often that your girlfriends refuse to hear about it anymore. Now you're going to have to get out of this relationship all by yourself, or make some new friends who don't realize that this is just a game you like to play.

Some Obvious Reasons to Get Out:

Your friends are all wondering what the hell is wrong with you,

If he was worth sticking around for in the first place, this vicious cycle would never have started,

Every moment you spend with the wrong guy is the opportunity missed to meet the right guy,

He's not the only man in town who's good in bed.

As a Call Out on the Carpet: "That song about 'the best part of breaking up is when you're making up' wasn't referring to crying wolf . . . she meant once!"

HUNGRY RABBIT

When you dump the guy you've been looking to discard for a while, and the sick bastard won't give up. **Be careful, girlfriend:** Incessant phone calls, unceasing flowers, and lovesick letters actually work on chicks.

Useful Tactics Include:

Using Caller ID to avoid his calls,

Writing "Return to Sender" on any mail that
    has his handwriting on it,

Telling him — not so softly — that this is a waste
    of time and that he should leave you alone,

Moving to another state.

As an Object of Obsession: "I've been screening my calls for weeks now — Hungry Rabbit is still trying to dig his way back in."

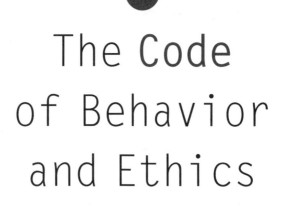

II

The Code
of Behavior
and Ethics

These are the life lessons, gathered over the years with your girlfriends, that amount to a code of honor shared by all. These lessons, about friendship, dating, and a few un-mentionables, are the kind of insider information that doesn't come in textbooks. Study hard, girls, there will be no makeup exam.

Girls' Night Out

"Play at your

own risk,

but

play to win."

— D.F.

WINGMAN

First thing to keep in mind when heading out to the front lines is, **Never Ever Leave Your Wingman**. Your wingman is the girl you plan and proceed through this night with. She is your eyes and ears when you're not looking and the one who will carry you back home if your ego or your liver is injured in battle. You are a team, out there in the trenches together. Go get 'em, girls.

DRESSING FOR BATTLE

Wingmen call each other up to discuss their ensembles before going out to the bar so they can be appropriately matched. After agreeing that you will wear a pantsuit and she will wear a sweater and skirt, it is not okay for either of you to show up in leather and high heels. As wingmen, you should be dressed to kill but also to complement each other. **P.S.** If your girlfriend breaks this code more than once, lose her; she doesn't want a friend, she wants someone to play Robin to her Batman.

FRUGALITY BEGETS FRUGALITY

If you don't like loaning your makeup, jewelry, shoes, or clothing, or anything else your wingman might want to borrow for girls' night out, then don't go asking for hers. If you want to play with her toys, you're going to have to share some of yours.

HEADING TO THE MINEFIELD

When two wingmen are driving to a drinking establishment and one girl already has a boyfriend to go home to, she drives. Reason no. 1: Single girl may need more alcohol to find herself a boy. Reason no. 2: Single girl may need to be dragged out of the bar by a friend who is not so desperate. When both girls are single, driving responsibilities should rotate or you should just go in the nicer of your two cars.

SCOPING

Like all good weekend warriors, wingmen looking for men
in bars need to do some reconnaissance. You and your
wingman should play a thorough game of "I spy" in shifts,
in sections, under false pretenses, under false names —
and don't forget under the table. But do it subtly, for that
is the art of the scope.

DOING LAPS

These are the circles wingmen make going around
and around and around the bar looking for their next
target. Later you will go around and around and around
the conversation, trying to figure out if he is right for you.
(And you thought the only exercise you got at the bar
was the eight-ounce curls.)

CALLING HIM

Girl A and Girl B sit at the bar. Girl A thinks guy in

blue sweater is cute and expresses this aloud to Girl B.

Girl A has just called him! He is now permanently

off-limits to Girl B.

Even if he begins chatting with Girl B, she can't go there

unless she wants to sacrifice the friendship.

TRANSFORMERS

These are the men you call that seem really attractive from

far away or before they open their mouths. But when they

come closer or begin to speak, they reveal that you called

them for no reason. Wingmen always reserve the right to

take a transformer off the list.

DON'T BE A BITCH

If your wingman hits it off with someone who seems attractive, don't subtly flirt with him to see if he would go for you instead. First off, there is nothing subtle about it — we all know what you're doing. Second, go get your own damn guy.

THE ALBATROSS

If you can't find your own guy to chat with, don't become a weight around your wingman's neck while she chats to hers. Pouting, yawning, complaining, or excessive blabbing will not get you invited back to girls' night out again.

ABANDONMENT

If you are the one chatting away with a guy, don't leave your wingman at the bar looking like prey. **For the Record:** After ninth grade, it's never cool to have long make-out sessions with your friend sitting next to you alone. Include your wingman in the conversation.

THE EXODUS

General Rule: Whenever possible, leave a bar at least thirty minutes before closing so no one is really sure how desperate you are. **Otherwise:** When Girl A wants to leave, give Girl B at least a fifteen-minute window. Girl B is allowed to ask for one extension of an additional fifteen minutes. When such time has elapsed, both girls must leave.

NO DIVIDE AND CONQUER

Remember the first rule? **Never Ever Leave Your Wingman ...** This counts at the end of the night also. Don't let your friend leave with a guy she just met, no matter how many drinks she has had.

Only Exceptions: If she runs into someone she is currently sleeping with or someone from the recycling bin (see "Stages"). Basically, don't let friends drive drunk, and this doesn't only apply to automobiles.

Making Your Move

"It's not

the having,

it's the

getting ."

— ELIZABETH TAYLOR

THROWING A RAP

When first meeting a guy, particularly if you have no long-term interest in him, **never let the truth get in the way of a good story.** As wingmen, you never contradict your friend's bullshit; rather, you should help her elaborate the tale as much as possible because if it gets her some, she will owe you big-time.

USING A CATCHER

The best wingman you could ask for is a girlfriend who is off the market. Married and otherwise committed team-mates can be your "catcher." Unlike real catchers, they screen prospective batters and help the good ones hit a home run. Very attractive catchers work two ways: First they interest people in the game, and later they have a built-in excuse to eject them if they strike out.

THE ASSESSMENT

When you're deciding whether you should make a pass at a man and you can't tell if he's interested, simply note how much time he's spending with you. If more than twenty-five minutes pass and you're still unable to greatly improve his job situation, he's interested, honey.

PIGEON-TOED DECISIONS

If you're still too chicken to roll the dice, remember this old standard: Men vote with their feet. If his shoes are pointed toward you, so is the thing in his trousers.

THROWING A FIRST-DEGREE PASS

The simplest and most casual way of asking a man out is to just offer him your number and remark how nice it would be if "you got together sometime for coffee." Not a big deal — even if he doesn't call — and odds are, he's still not sure whether you're truly interested. **P.S.** And it doesn't matter at all if you don't drink coffee.

DATES BEFORE 5 P.M.

Setting up lunches, coffees, museums, or walks through the park are wonderful ways to start a slow-motion courtship. It sets a boundary — and implies you're not interested in "nighttime activities" until further notice.

THROWING A SECOND-DEGREE PASS

Calling a man, rather than waiting for him to call you, is more to the point. This helps you figure out where you stand within five days, because if he returns the call and makes the date, you know he's game.

PHONE RATIONS

If he calls you first and you're trying to decide how long to wait before calling him back, keep the following in mind: Call whenever the hell you want.

Unless you're dating a man in Los Angeles: Then double the amount of time it took *him* to call *you.*

SELECTED DIALING

However, if a man has called you once for a date and you call him within the first hour of his message to you or try him like a desperado all day long until you get him on the phone, the pass will be fouled out.

THROWING A THIRD-DEGREE PASS

This would be asking a man to come home with you. If you're not intending to sleep with him, you want to make that clear before you leave together. But if your intention is to hook up, you just saved yourself a lot of time.

GOING IN FOR THE KILL

Although it's usually the man who attempts kissing you first, and initiating everything that comes afterward, if he's circling too long before taking the plunge, feel free to take matters into your own hands. Short-term, you may risk emasculating him; long-term, neither of you will care.

A WORD ON BEER GOGGLES

Be aware that alcohol can impair your vision and judgment so badly that you may not realize you're making moves on a cretin or sociopath. This is the time to go back to your wingman and trust her if she tells you to move on. **Remember:** Two eyes are always better than none in the bar.

First Date
Forget-Me-Nots

"The thing you want

the most in life will be the hardest

thing you ever do, so you might

as well shoot big."

— PATRICIA FARR (MY MOTHER)

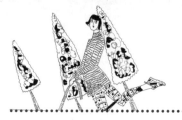

TRUST YOUR INSTINCTS

Women's intuition works in one direction only: If you think he's a good guy, you might be wrong ... but if you think he's a bad guy, you are most definitely right.

FIRST-DATE "IN CASES"

First: Have your own transportation and your own cash in case everything goes wrong.

Second: Have three prepared questions and three rehearsed stories in case the conversation lapses.

Third: Have an escape plan — somewhere you have to be (really early) in the morning — in case you need an emergency exit.

THE NUMBERS GAME

If he has your home phone number, don't give him
the address. If he has your work number, don't give
him your home one. If he takes you out of town
for the day, ask for a phone number where people can
reach you. If he thinks you're weird, then maybe he isn't.
It's always better to be safe than sorry.

ZONING LAWS

On your first date, your hands communicate the important messages.

Touching between the wrist and the biceps are signs
of warmth, yet not leading.

Touching the inside of hand, cheek, neck, and feet
are considered making a move.

Touching the lower thigh, top of hand, waist, or back
of head are just plain confusing.

Any place not mentioned indicates you want to have
sex within the hour.

TAKE 'EM OFF THE MENU

There are many food items you should avoid on first dates.

Here's a quick guide of things to skip:

Italian: No linguine, cappelline, or fettuccine

Pizza: Toppings are not your friend

Indian: Those foods with awesome powers over your bowels that may take effect before you get home

Seafood: Any crustacean that requires you to use your hands in order to eat it

BLUE BLOODS

When you ask your date where he went to college and instead of a name he tells you, "New York, New Jersey, Connecticut, or Boston," it means he went to an Ivy League school.

The following rules apply:

Do not drink white wine with dinner,

Do not have more than two glasses of red,

Do not sleep with him for at least three months, and

Do not talk about nude photos of yourself

POWER MATING

When your dinner conversation feels more like a job interview and you sense that he is trying to decide if your assets will enhance his social or financial portfolio enough that he should bother to take himself off the market, run for the door: Dating is not supposed to be a power struggle. You lose this one even when you win.

CHECK DIPLOMACY

On the first date, it's always best to offer to pay for half, for several reasons:

(1) If you want to be an equal, then you should act like one

(2) It calms his fears about needy women

(3) If he lets you, you know you should probably just get out now

(4) It keeps him wondering whether or not you're interested

THE UGLY UNDERWEAR RULE

If you really want to hook up on a first date, wear your ugliest underwear. Inevitably, you'll hook up.

THE UNSHAVEN LEGS RULE

If you apply this and the ugly underwear rule at the same time, you'll probably marry the guy.

R.K.

When the date is over and you think you like him but you're still not exactly sure, a little **R**ecreational **K**issing probably won't hurt him or you. **And** . . . it may help answer that question of whether you're interested.

I.R.K.

Irresponsible Recreational Kissing is when you make out with him because you foolishly think you have to or when you already know you're not interested and just aren't mature enough to say so.

PICK UP AFTER YOURSELF

If a girlfriend was kind enough to loan you an outfit for this important evening out, make sure you dry-clean it immediately. Don't keep it, thinking you have some nostalgic right to adopt it. Return it — cleaned — by next weekend, or you could karmicly damage the date you just had. (Not really, but return her damn clothes anyway.)

Rules of the Wild

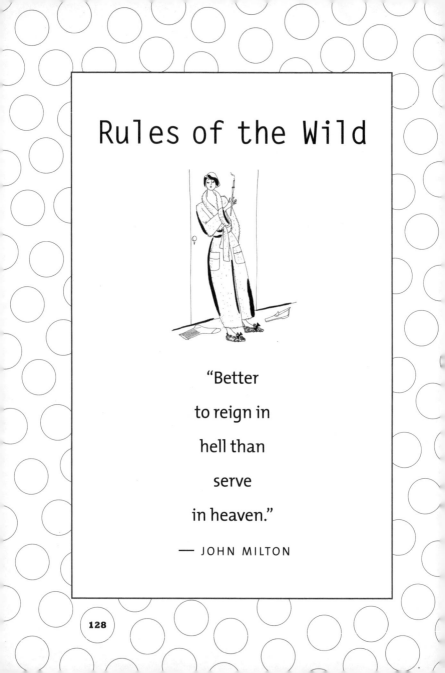

"Better

to reign in

hell than

serve

in heaven."

— JOHN MILTON

LOOSE WOMEN 101

If you want a one-night stand with any man, at any time, for any reason, if it's cool with you — then more power to you. But let's go over the basics:

(1) Don't expect a meaningful relationship with him afterward

(2) Don't expect the sex to be above average

(3) If he's been your good friend for a long time, you can pretty much kiss the friendship good-bye

(4) Don't get emotional about him just before, midway through, or ever after

(5) Don't bother wasting any time regretting it

NO-SPOONING ZONE

If you take a guy home and have your way with him immediately, do not attempt to curl up and cuddle afterward. Men don't like cuddling anyway; he certainly doesn't want to bother with the warrior princess who just slayed him.

SLUMBER-FREE ZONE

One-night stands are not slumber parties, ladies; this was about one thing only. You weren't invited to sleep over, so get while the getting's good.

THE REVOLVING DOOR

If you brought him home to your house, don't be afraid to show him the door when you're done. Nice girls can ask a man to leave. Smile as you say: "Don't let the door hit you on the ass on the way out."

LIMB SNACKING

When you fail to follow the rules of leaving immediately, you will wake up in the morning and realize that you now have to chew your arm off to sneak out without waking the beast. **No matter what,** they never look as good in the morning.

THE WALK OF SHAME

As every college graduate knows, this is the stroll home after your indecent act, which everyone who sees you knows you just committed, because you're in some outfit that reeks of "I wore this ensemble last night . . . and am just going home now." It's usually accentuated by a hairdo that looks the same.

SEXUAL HANGOVER

You know the guilt that accompanies excessive drinking? Multiply it times ten, and now you know what to expect the day after a one-night stand. **P.S.** This hangover doesn't go away as fast as the drinking kind.

MERCY F**K

When you've held out for so long that you actually take pity on the man before breaking off your sexless relationship, so you just give him a piece of the pie, so to speak, before letting him go.

REBOUND RUN-IN

When you've been broken up with a guy for a really long time, and you just happen to see him out somewhere. Do all the catching up you want until you sleep with him; then just consider yourselves all caught up and move on.

LOVE SLAVE

If you see any man (including an ex-boyfriend) on a number of occasions, over any length of time, for one purpose only. Even though it's a common occurrence, in spirit it counts as a one-night stand.

HOWEVER

If you sleep with a guy on a first date, it does not necessarily constitute a one-night stand. You may go on to have a long-term relationship. Then again, he could change his opinion of you after having sex so soon ... but then what the hell would you want with him anyway.

Shopping at
the Mall

"Iago was nothing

compared to some of the women

I went to high school with."

— D.F.

NO SIMULTANEOUS TRY-ONS

Never ever try on the same article of clothing that your friend is trying on. At best, this causes insecurity in both parties. At worst, it inspires an unnecessary and false sense of hubris in one friend and anywhere from three days to three weeks of depression in the other.

GETTING A PERMISSION SLIP

If your girlfriend purchases an article of clothing and you will absolutely die without it, you must ask her permission before buying it for your own collection. **Warning:** Do not attempt to buy the article and rationalize that you will never wear it in her presence, because *you know* you will run into her one evening when you're both wearing it.

STIPULATIONS TO PERMISSION SLIPS

(1) When verbally applying for a permission slip, you must solemnly swear that you will always clear it with her when you want to wear the article.

(2) You must also affirm that you will always give credit where credit is due and tell any mutual friend who compliments you that she had it first.

CLONING

When you realize that you're buying item number three that your friend already owns, you are now officially a clone of your friend. If you find yourself in this situation, it is time to stop shopping and go get a therapist. (And just so you know, her friends call you a loser behind your back.)

AVOIDING THE CLAWS

Wherever possible, try to shop with a friend who has a relatively similar body type and a relatively similar wallet size. Too many hours in a department store with women who are excessively thin or excessively rich can drive even the kindest girl to random acts of violence.

BARNYARD DRESSING ROOMS

You know those communal fitting rooms that force you to change your clothes in front of everyone else? The ones with no privacy and not even a curtain to hide behind?

Don't shop there.

First of all, you all look like a bunch of cows grazing on marked-down items. Second, it's hard to feel fabulous in a potential new dress with naked people around you. **General Rule:** Naked will always upstage you.

VICTORIA'S OTHER SECRET

Don't go underwear shopping with your girlfriends.
It's just weird.

SANDAL-READY FEET

If your friend hasn't learned the importance of a pedicure,
don't let her go trying on strappy little sling backs. Keep
her moving toward the tall boot section no matter what
... or you will be the one explaining why even the sales-
men keep their distance.

COAT CLUSTERS

The only time it is okay to have the same coat as your friend
is when you are on the same sports team, in the same sorority, or working together at the same company and they
were free. **Automatic Exceptions:** when you're sleeping
with men who are on the same team, in the same fraternity,
or working for the same company.

MI CASA NO ES TU CASA

Don't buy your friends decorative items for their homes. Your taste is not their taste, and they can't even return your gifts if they don't like them because they know you are going to look for them when you come over.

QUICK CUTS

It is never cool to have the same haircut as your friend. Similar can be cute; the same practically implies lesbianism. **And while you're at it:** Don't get your hair cut at the mall anyway.

ANIMALS "Я" US

Don't go to those pet stores in the mall with fellow females. You already know it makes you smell like cat litter for the rest of the day, but you may not know what two women together in a pet store also stink of: impending spinsterhood.

Wedding Party Politics

"Old

friendship

does

not rust."

— HENRIK IBSEN

FIRST-ROUND DRAFTS

In case everyone has forgotten, the bride-to-be picks her bridesmaids because they are close friends, not because they're a perfect size six. If you skip your closest friends, for the ones who look prettiest in photos, no one will ever be over to see them.

UNIFORM HELL

The time to think about a bridesmaid's dress size is when you are choosing the dress. Putting a size fourteen-plus friend in a pink sequin sweetheart neck with no sleeves will be seen as an act of aggression, not friendship.
If you make your bridesmaids look like a sideshow, they're going to steal your spotlight, to both of your dismay.

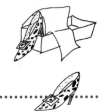

SOME PERSPECTIVE

Though brides want to believe that their bridesmaids
will do differently, no one ever wears their dress again.
We don't shorten it, we won't redye the shoes, and usually
the whole ensemble takes up valuable closet space
for up to five years. So never kid yourself, it's destined
for the garbage.

A THOUSAND-DOLLAR WEEKEND

The outfit your bridesmaids will love you for is the one
they don't spend a lot of money on. **How much is too
much?** Decide which bridesmaid in your party makes
the least amount of money, estimate her daily take, and
multiply by two. That's how much she should pay for
the tent and tires she has to buy and wear on your important day.

HONOR AMONG MAIDS

All weddings have glitches and all wedding parties are dysfunctional, and the maid of honor is honorbound to keep the bride in the dark. **For instance:** Control the details, organize the shopping, edit the backstabbing, and keep her mother as far away from her as you can.

IT'S NOT A EULOGY

In recent years, maids of honor have started giving toasts at receptions and have subsequently been screwing it up as much as the best men ever did. **Handy Tip:** Keep in mind that Nana doesn't need to know little details like how many people the bride slept with before this fool, when this couple really consummated their relationship, or insider bets on when the divorce will be.

Keep it light and fluffy, girls.

STRIP-CLUB TRYOUTS

The dance floor at a wedding reception is not boogie wonderland. You're in a dress, act like a lady.

DID YOU NOTICE THE COCKTAIL RECEPTION ALSO SERVES FOOD?

Pacing your liquor intake at weddings is key to remaining friends with the couple afterward. Most people getting married these days are over twenty-one years old; you should know how to drink by now. Too much liquid and not enough substance will have you passing out on Aunt Peggy or Uncle Joe.

PINK TAFFETA PUNCHES

The tossing of the bouquet is not a championship face-off of single women. And very likely, the woman you body-check will be standing next to you at next year's wedding, too. It's just a ritual, not a rite of passage ... let it go.

BEAR TRAPS

When you are about to hook up with a groomsman early on at the event, ask yourself a few important questions before proceeding. **For instance:** Do you have a date coming later who will surely find out? Does he have a date coming later who may endanger your ridiculous bridesmaid hairdo? **And more to the point:** Is he hot enough to do it anyway?

KEEP YOUR DRESS ON HERE!

Number one thing to keep in mind:

DO NOT HOOK UP IN THE WEDDING SUITE.

Not in the bathroom, not in the chair, not on the floor, and, dear Lord, not in the bed. Not even if the wedding is your sister's, your best friend's, or even your mother's. **And while you're at it:** Stay out of the limos, too.

Lines to
Never Cross

"Men are like buses . . . you sit
at the stop long enough and another one comes along — but girlfriends are like Maseratis:
few and far between." — D.F.

GIRLFRIENDS ARE THICKER
THAN BOYFRIENDS

There is NEVER EVER any good reason to get involved
with your friend's boyfriend. Just as oil is thicker
than water, and the two don't mix well, the same goes
for a friendship with her and crossing the line with him.
This is the essence of being a girl's girl.

The song was wrong . . . stand by your *friend*.

NOSE PICKING

Remember the old saying "It's okay to pick your nose, and
it's okay for your friend to pick her nose, but it's not okay
to pick . . . ," the same applies here:

You can date your old boyfriend's friend, **but you can
never date your friend's old boyfriend.** No matter when
they broke up, stay away. **Remember:** He may not still be
hers in fact, but he should always be hers in anecdote.

DON'T SHOP IN OTHER PEOPLE'S CLOSETS

Say you meet a man and he likes you but has some girlfriend that you don't know and probably never will:
there is still no reason to go there.

First of all: If he really liked you, he would free himself
from her before pursuing you.

Second: If he'll cheat on her, he'll probably cheat on you.

Third: He believes the same of you.

Last but not least: Karma is a real and powerful thing that
doesn't only exist in Tibet.

··

IN-CASE-OF-EMERGENCY BOYFRIEND

This is that guy friend of yours who you secretly know is just waiting around for the day you give up on the dating scene and just date him . . . because he's sure if you gave him a chance, you could actually like him "that way."
You know you will never like him "that way" — why screw up the friendship?

IN-CASE-OF-EMERGENCY HUSBAND

This is a different guy friend of yours, with whom you share an unspoken pact that if both of you get to a "certain age" and neither of you has found someone, that you'll just marry each other.
Yeah, that's a healthy idea.

CLEARANCE-RACK SPECIALS

This is the guy you dated years ago who checks in every so often to see if you're finally ready to settle for his crap. Usually, he also has the gumption to tell you that his crap hasn't changed, but it's still on sale for you, at the same special rate. What a bargain!

THE FAG HAG PHILOSOPHY

This is the gay guy you are secretly in love with that you sit around waiting for the day he suddenly wakes up and realizes he can't be gay because you're so damn fabulous for him! Yeah right, that might happen.

KNOW YOUR RATIO

When you've been dating the same man for a while and
need to decide when to pay, employ this ratio:

Struggling artist or college student:

He pays for one and you pay for one.

Between twenty-two and twenty-eight years old and

wears a suit: He pays for three and you pay for one.

Anyone over thirty who's not in recovery:

He pays for five and you pay for one.

Anyone more than eight years your senior or over forty:

He pays.

DOUBLES

Double dates were created for people who are bored of talking to each other. There's no need to bother with them until you have reached such a point. But when you get there ...

Refrain from:

Excessive chatting with the other man at the table,

Taking potshots at your date for the other couple's
amusement,

Relentlessly describing dietary needs or overwhelming
the waitress by rewriting the menu.

YOUR TEAM

When you're out with your friends and bringing
your man along, remember to:

Limit conversations about the old days when you were
slutting around,

Make him feel as though he is wanted here,

Leave a little room for him to shine.

HIS TEAM

When you're out with his friends it is not a time to see
how many shots you can do; nor should you:

Wear leather,

Flirt with his guy friends,

Confide in his girlfriends (as they will report back to him),

Henpeck, dominate the conversation, or insist on paying.

BEGGING

If you are involved with a man who won't give you the
commitment that you want dump him, kill him, or just
get over it, but don't beg. It won't do you any good, and
you ruin the reputations of all the rest of us.

Tests

"It is a curious thought,
but it is only when you see people
looking ridiculous that you realize
just how much you love them."

— AGATHA CHRISTIE

THE WAITRESS TEST

On your first date with a man, go to dinner and watch
how he treats the waitress. **Wanna know why?**
Because in six months this is just how he will treat
you. The waitress is a "given," and she will try to appease
him no matter how he treats her … which may one
day apply to you. **Apply This Also to:** his mother, a cashier,
the mechanic, and ex-lovers. **This does not apply to:** his
dog — and don't be fooled by his display of loyalty here.

THE DOG TEST

Men will test you with their dogs, which they subcon-
sciously consider an extension of their penises. Stroke it,
pet it, play rough, and move on.

Never Ever: Cuddle with it or talk baby talk to it …
even if he does.

Also Refrain from: buying toys for the animal too early
on; it's too obvious and your cover will be blown.

THE DOORBELL TEST

On your second or third date, ask him to pick you up at your home. If he stays in his car and honks, don't even think of leaving the house. You wait, like the debutante you are, until he rings the doorbell and presents himself, just like the days when they had to impress Mom and Dad.

Never stray from this because: If you jump when he honks, you will one day jump when he barks (as in, "Bring me the chicken pot pie, bitch.")

If He Asks if You Heard Him Honk: "Oh, I didn't think you were calling for me; I just assumed you were having trouble parking."

THE CAR DOOR TEST

Well-mannered men will walk to the car and open your door first. As they walk around to their door, recognize that they are actually testing *you:* Do you unlock it for them, or do you fail to be considerate?

First off: If he doesn't open your side first, you stand there and wait, if necessary until he drives away.

Second: Just unlock the door and pass his damn test, even if you don't care about him; you should never fail anything.

THE EX TEST

Early on in the game, make some casual inquiries about his ex. Your sole purpose here is to find out how he will one day speak about you.

Run for the door if:

The words *restraining order* come up,

He tells you her most personal secret,

He says he still loves her or explains that modeling for the Victoria Secret catalog took up too much of her time.

If he refuses to discuss her: That may not be such a bad thing ... you've got an interesting one at least.

THE FAMILY TEST

The first time a potential boyfriend brings you to his family home, remember your manners, look virginal, and pretend there's nothing riding on this encounter. But don't fail to take this opportunity to see how he relates to them. Remember, this is how he plans on playing house one day down the road.

Things to pick up on:

If Mom still cuts his meat,

Three hundred bottles of beer on the wall,

If there are snapshots of his ex-girlfriend all over the house,

If Dad is nice to his wife.

But do give him some slack: After all, everyone's family is crazy.

Kinds of Love

My mother

always told me

there are

three kinds

of love . . .

Some People Are: **IN LOVE**

The amazing, blessed state that few people actually achieve. Occurs in women who have found their: soul mate, life partner, unfailing confidant, eternal livable roommate, other half, permanent designated driver, and forever best friend.

For most, this is found only: in children's books, once in a lifetime, after years of therapy, and after a few test runs in short-term markets.

CAUTION: The only way to know for sure is after fifty years of life together.

But More People Are: **IN LOVE WITH LOVE**

Which occurs during the initial period of a relationship when you do actually hear birds singing and all that crap. You have no need to sleep, you have a feeling in your bones that resembles a drug-induced high, and the guy still really likes your family. **But before you call this love, ask yourself these questions:**

Have you seen anything but his best behavior?

Has he seen yours?

Would you like him 100 pounds heavier with no hair?

Is this the senility patient for you?

Until you're sure: Let's face it, you are "in Like."

And Sadly More People Are:

IN LOVE WITH THE DRAMA

The drama arises from the never-ending chase, the never surrendering heart you wish to attain, the never fixable qualities you're convinced you can fix, or the never-ending problems you are resolved to overcome.

Well, Wake Up and:

Stop trying to fix your dad,

Start thinking more of yourself, or no one else will,

Stop riding roller coasters and opt for a sit and spin.

Instead: Spend six months celibate, go dancing with girlfriends, get a hobby, and eventually you'll get a real life.

I Have Also Found These Kinds of Love . . .

IN LOVE WITH THE CIRCLE

When you can't separate the crowd or the lifestyle
from the man you are dating.

Kind of like when the sundress in the window looks so
good with the necklace, the boots, the gloves, and the hat,
but when you get it home alone, it's a tacky piece of shit.

Things to Assess:

If you sat at a bus stop for the evening, would you enjoy
his company?

If you had no money to spend on a date, what would
you do?

Do you ever talk about anything substantial?

Do you secretly have a crush on his best friend?

Beware of a Good Rationalization: They just perpetuate
the situation.

IN LOVE WITH THE PAYCHECK

Needing little explanation, symptoms of this kind of love can include liking a man for his money, clothing, position, favorite restaurant, vacation home, frequent flyer miles, or anything else that calls for his platinum card.

Keep in Mind: Rich men have a tendency to go back to their high school sweetheart, and money doesn't give you taste, personality, or empathy . . . nor does it make a man.

Treatment for this Ailment: You might consider inflating your own income first and looking into men afterward.

IN LOVE WITH THE TIMING

When feelings of love are falsely induced by the "appropri-ateness" of the time in your life. Usually occurs during senior year of high school or college, second year of a real job, six months before the thirtieth birthday, or whenever the biological clock starts ticking.

Beware of: feeling as if you missed out on things later in life if your timing is early and knowing the difference

between your timing and your mother's influence.

Also Note: Timing may contribute to a lasting relationship nonetheless, and without this kind of love, most of us would never have been born.

IN LOVE WITH THE SEX

Works best when he doesn't have deep feelings for you, either. Keep in mind that this kind of love is the most difficult to sustain and the most destructive to your head.

For the Record: You might believe that adding some exciting stuff to your sexual repertoire is worth putting up with an unhealthy relationship because you think you can always bring these new tricks to a real relationship later — but you can't. *Reality Says:* The longer you romp on this futon, the longer it will take to find a real bed.

Chick Tricks

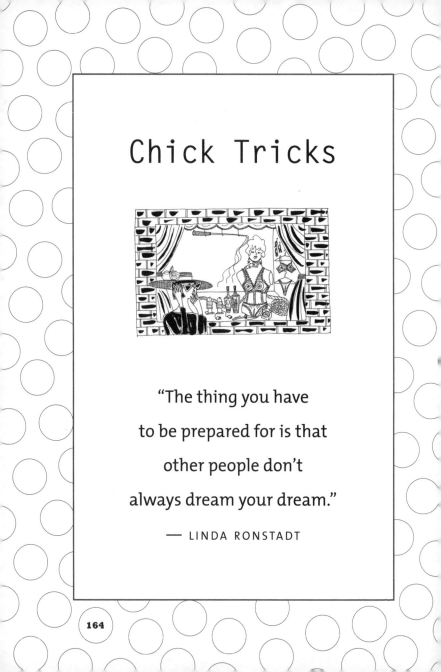

"The thing you have
to be prepared for is that
other people don't
always dream your dream."

— LINDA RONSTADT

TABLE FOR ONE

If you fall into the unfortunate category of women who can't reach orgasm — and your friends aren't talking — start going to bed early until you can burn the candle at both ends, all by yourself.

SEEK AND YE SHALL FIND

Invest some time alone, figuring out what works for you. Education begins at home, and this kind of homework really pays off later. **Keep in Mind:** After high school, it's cool to do your homework.

CHOOSING A MAJOR

Just like freshman year of college — start by trying everything that might interest you. You can decide your main course of study closer to graduation.

BATHROOM STUDIES 101

Every single woman needs to have a shower massager.

Because it's detachable.

(A word to the not-so-wise: Watch the water

temperature, honey.)

BUYING A BOYFRIEND

Go to the adult toy store, with three straightfaced

girlfriends if necessary, and purchase plastic boyfriend

parts, with batteries or without.

(Ask for something with "rabbit ears."

Don't ask why, just ask for it.)

DANGER, WILL ROBINSON!

Keep in Mind:

Ultimately, intercourse is not supposed to remain a one-

person sport. (These are an aid, ladies, not a life partner.)

FINDING A TUTOR

There also exists the kind of man that will teach you everything you ever needed to know about your own physiology, but had no idea of what to ask. If you're lucky enough to run across one, be a good student.

SPECIAL ED CLASSES

If you are looking for some suggestions, answers, explanations or information, remember that videos, movies, cable television, and the Internet aren't just for thirteen-year-old boys.

THE GOLDEN RULE

Never fake it.

No matter how hard you're trying to achieve orgasm, there is no need and no reason to **ever** fake it.

This does neither you nor your partner any good.

III

The Boy Code

A few words about how the other half lives, and how the other team plays . . . so you can be a more informed opponent.

What They Say

"Some men are like martinis:
ice cold and very dry, but they think
they're the best drink in the house
because of the two olives they've
got stuck on the end of their
swizzle stick." — D.F.

....

TAINT

On the male body, the small space between the testicles and the anus, eloquently named by sophomoric men, because "it-ain't one and it-ain't the other."

Good to Know Because:

All men are ticklish here,

If you apply pressure to it, they will do anything you ask,

The naming of it alone shows insight to what men
discuss in locker rooms,

It's a guy thing we shouldn't even know about.

As a Place: "You're not ticklish? Yeah, what about your taint? Right ... here!"

DUTCH OVEN

This is when you're in bed with a man and he farts under the covers. If you're dating a freshman, he may pull the covers over your head so you really get the full effect.

If You Allow This Behavior:

Expect it to become part of your foreplay,

Accept the fact that you are a substitute
   for his little brother,

Know that he will try other regression tactics on you,

Get ready to watch your sex drive disappear.

As a Boundary to Maintain: "Yeah, I find a Dutch oven funny, as funny as you not gettin' any this week."

....

C**K BLOCK

This is a term men use to describe anything that gets

in the way of hooking up with a woman.

It Can Be:

His personal history or yours,

His drinking or yours,

His biological functions or yours,

But Most Often It's:

His friend or yours.

Don't Allow Him to: Make this a pet name for your parents

or best friend.

HEISMAN

This is a guy term used to describe when a woman keeps a
man at arms-length distance and denies him love or sex
or whatever it is that he wants. The name comes from college football's Heisman Trophy, which features a player
stiff-arming an imaginary opponent.

Don't Give Up This Status:

It means you have the ball in your court,

He will run up and down that field all day trying
    to achieve his goal,

This is the most effort you will ever get out of this guy,

The best victories come after beating someone
    at his own game.

As Music to Your Ears: "The chick's had me in a full Heisman
all week, and she is one worthy opponent."

SPINNER

This is a term used by men to describe a petite woman. The term implies that if the male were standing up during sex, this small woman could be spun around in circles without touching the floor. (Isn't that nice?)

Just When You Thought:

We had evolved from the apes,

"Short people got no reason to live" was as mean as it gets,

He asked you to wear those shoes because they made
your legs look nice,

You might have been too rough on an ex-boyfriend.

If It's Used in Your Presence: "She may be a spinner, darling, but your penis would have to be a little bigger to achieve such acrobatics."

BIRD DOG

A term that men use to describe other men who cheat. This is one to pay particular attention to, because if a man thinks another man is a dog to women, then he's really got to be pretty awful.

Keep in Mind:

Men are much bigger gossips than women,
    and they know the real story,
Men who cheat blatantly enough to deserve the name
    are not candidates for rehabilitation,
Men who use the term in reference to another might
    themselves be someone to consider,
They might have used it just to get you to consider them.

To Spell It Out for You: "A bird dog is not just a male slut, he's a slut who lies, cheats, and steals and is messy about it to boot."

HALL PASS

This term is used by men to jeer a buddy who has a girl in his life. It implies that he who is involved has to check with his woman before going out with his friends, because she keeps his testicles in a lockbox and he needs permission to get them back.

Which in Turn Implies:

That his friends think he is a loser,

That the woman is the evil schoolmarm who is afraid
  to let the boy out of the classroom,

    or

Such a strong girl that her man's afraid he'll lose
  her if she's on her own for fifteen minutes.

If He Asks You for One Directly: Tell him some people get detention so much because they ask for it.

What They Do

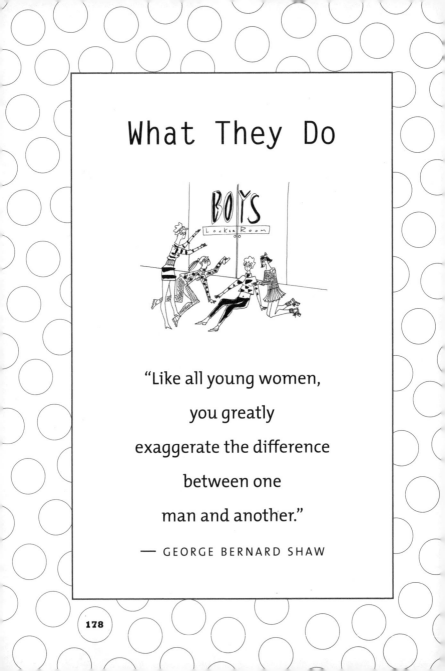

"Like all young women,

you greatly

exaggerate the difference

between one

man and another."

— GEORGE BERNARD SHAW

MEMBERS ONLY

There are men you will date who are still members of the "old boys' school" and have their own codes of honor that they don't reveal to women. It doesn't necessarily mean that he's a bad guy, it just means that he's a guy's guy. So keep the following in mind ...

A SPORTING MAN'S MOTIVATIONS

Men and sports evolve with age, and each stage has its own rules:

High school guys play sports for their fathers'
    approval as well as the cheerleaders,
College men play sports for the free education,
    the parties, the camaraderie, and the cheerleaders,
Postgraduate boys play sports to find friends, deny hair
    loss, do something with their anger at their boss,
    and prove to their girlfriends that they used to
    date cheerleaders.

COUCH JOCKS

Men who have retired from sports bond around the television and compete by commentating on sports. They earn points by second-guessing the announcer and getting ready to coach Little League, where they will avoid the cheerleaders they married and admire the ones they can no longer have.

LOCKER ROOM LOOKS

The only reason men believe women are worried about "size" is that men themselves are obsessed with it. Since their early days in school, men "size" one another up in locker rooms and worry over themselves whenever they get the chance. It's like women talking about weight: Don't get involved.

CREDENTIALS

Men judge one another by these three simple things:
the watch on his wrist, the shoes on his feet, and the girl
on his arm. (But before you get insulted, it's just like certain women in suburbia, who judge one another by the
kind of car in the driveway, how big the house behind it is,
and the sucker inside who bought it all for her.)

BOYS' NIGHT OUT

Men have a drinking code that differs from ours.
Try not to interfere with the following, as it's part
of the whole "hunter/gatherer thing":
Never refuse a shot (or else be considered weak),
If a guy or crew of guys buys a man a drink, he must buy
    at least the same number of drinks for them,
However, picking up too many rounds in front of the
    other men's dates is wrongfully ostentatious (and in
    some places just cause for a punch in the mouth).

RAT PACKS

When mingling in the bar scene, men will have no respect
for women who:

Come right out and ask them to buy drinks,

Swear, spit, or swallow more cocktails than they do,

Wear clothing that is too small for their bodies — if they
don't have the body to carry it,

Make passes at other men while their boyfriends are
in the bathroom, without a warning that the
boyfriends are coming back.

RELATIONSHIP ATTIRE

If a man asks you to wear a particular outfit when
you're going out to meet his friends, know this is intended
to signal to his friends his level of interest in you.
Understand the rules and dress accordingly:
Hat on backwards and jeans = a friend he's trying
to seem casual about until he gets their approval.

Shirt two sizes too small = just a bimbo he's doing,

or a hotty he's trying to impress them with.

Well-made power suit = girl he aspires to date regularly,

marry, or be kept by.

Simple dress that makes her look either sexy or like the

girl next door = the one they should all be vying for.

FIRSTS ARE FOREVER

If you tell a man he is your first, after ninth grade he will automatically assume you're lying. If you manage to convince him otherwise, he will treasure it forever. (So if you do lie about your virginity and make an ass of him, he'll probably spend eternity trying to make one of you.)

ONCE HAD, TWICE SHY

If you've already dated a guy in a circle of friends and now you find yourself fancying another one in the same circle, odds are he may not go for you. **However**, men are more disloyal about sex than anything else, so if you really want him, persistence will pay off.

BLOCK BUSTERS

If you've been around the block with more than two guys in the same crowd, guy number three or more in the crew will never be your boyfriend. This new man you engage in this posse is there only for the action: because men will torture the hell out of one another for dating a woman the rest of his mates know all too well.

INTEREST POINTS

When a man is interested in a relationship, there are three kinds of dates that let you know:

Dinner for two: because he wouldn't listen to you for ninety minutes unless he really wanted to,

Meeting the family: because he wouldn't get them excited unless he thought there was good reason,

His favorite sporting event: because he wouldn't risk this heartfelt pastime with someone who could possibly ruin it.

The Mother Code

The following is the Pledge of Allegiance to The Girl Code. If Moses was a woman under that tunic, I think these would have come from the Almighty One.

Learn them and live by them.

The
Top Five
Laws
of
The Girl
Code

5. RECIPROCAL THERAPY

If your heart is broken and your girlfriend spends hours trying to put it back together, find a way to reciprocate, in whatever way is meaningful to her. Girlfriends always deserve to be repaid for their efforts (whether it's helping organize her closet or buying her the little dress she could have picked out for herself while she was helping you). When you don't bother to return her favors, it's not friend-ship — it's freeloading.

4. "THERE BUT BY THE GRACE OF GOD GO I"

A little reminder about bashing your fellow females: Before you verbally slam a sister, remember that you can't judge her unless you've walked in her shoes. We need to stand up for one another, or no one else will. Be a good teammate.

3. NEVER COUNT

If you don't know how many men you slept with, it will
never get you into trouble. If a man asks, you don't know. If
he insists, tell him it is against The Girl Code to reply.

2. DON'T BET THE FARM

It is never good or plentiful to date your girlfriends'
boyfriends, ex-boyfriends, crushes, long-term attractions, or
brothers, because the odds are against you that she will ever
be your friend afterward, even if you marry one of them.

1. NEVER BETRAY THE T-SHIRT COLLECTION SOCIETY

All women know that we secretly collect men's garb, until we marry them, at which point it's all ours anyway. This starts in high school with varsity jackets, progresses in college to all sporting attire (highest points going to sweatshirts), and postcollege to man-tailored shirts, suit jackets, and eventually socks. Never admit that we compare, collect, and grade our wins.

In closing, ladies,
I leave you with one last quote:

"A woman is like a tea bag:
you can't see how strong she is
until you see her in hot water."

— ELEANOR ROOSEVELT

And one sentence of advice: *The only thing you really
need to get through anything in life is girlfriends
— value them accordingly.*

Go get your dreams, girls.